Walk Your Way To Weight Loss

LINDSEY PYLARINOS

The Ultimate Guide On How To Lose Weight, Burn Fat & Stay Thin With Walking

2nd Edition

Walk Your Way To Weight Loss

Copyright 2014 by Lindsey Pylarinos - All rights reserved.

In no way is it legal to reproduce, duplicate, or transmit any part of this document in either electronic means or in printed format. Recording of this publication is strictly prohibited and any storage of this document is not allowed unless with written permission from the publisher. All rights reserved.

Table of Contents

Introduction 5

Chapter 1 – Understanding the Role of Walking in Losing Weight 6

Chapter 2 – Six Scientific Facts About Walking 15

Chapter 3 – Why Walk Your Way to Weight Loss? 27

Chapter 4 – Before Starting Your Walking Program 30

Chapter 5 – Your Walking Form 38

Chapter 6 – Walking Your Way Towards Weight Loss 42

Chapter 7 – Walk This Way, Walk That Way 46

Chapter 8 – More Smart Walking Ideas 49

Chapter 9 - Using Pedometer in Walking to Shape Up and Slim Down 54

Chapter 10 – Walking to Lose Weight Success Stories 58

Chapter 11 – Walking Workout Plans and How it Works 64

Chapter 12 - Additional Facts About Walking 75

Chapter 13 - Joining a Walking Club 80

Conclusion 89

Check Out My Other Books 90

Introduction

I want to thank you and congratulate you for purchasing the book, "Walk Your Way to Weight Loss – The Ultimate Guide On How to Lose Weight, Burn Fat, and Stay Thin With Walking".

This book contains proven steps and strategies on how to walk it all off towards your weight loss goals.

The book contains tips and perspectives on how to use walking as the best, and at the same time easiest and cheapest way to lose that unwanted weight for a healthier life and wellbeing.

Thanks again for purchasing this book, I hope you enjoy it!

Chapter 1 – Understanding the Role of Walking in Losing Weight

Walking is free, easy and one of the simplest ways to lose weight, get more active and become healthier. It is an underrated form of exercise. It is ideal for people of all ages and fitness levels who want to become healthier and more active. Aside from helping people in losing weight, walking has been very effective in reducing the risk of chronic illnesses, like type 2 diabetes, heart disease, stroke, asthma and some cancers.

Types of Walking

There are two basic types of walking: racewalking and power-walking (also referred to as speed-walking). Racewalking is an Olympic sport with rules, while power-walking is carried out more recreationally. For instance, there's a rule in racewalking that the back toe of the athlete should not leave the ground until the front foot has come into contact with the ground. Both types are excellent forms of workout that yield health and fitness benefits.

Technique is not necessary with the other type of walking. All you need to do is to get out and walk. This is known as the plain old walking technique, one step in front of the other. People have been doing it from the time they have learned their first step. Experts suggest that a person should learn the technique in walking to help him lose weight and become healthier.

Walking Techniques Every Individual Should Know

Legwork

1. One of the most common mistakes beginners commit when trying to walk fast is lengthening the stride or overstriding. This mistake is biomechanically inefficient and can slow you down. Because it is inefficient, it can burn more calories, but you may burn less calories overall because you cannot walk far due to fatigue.
2. Instead of lengthening the stride of walking to walk faster, focus on a powerful push off while the front foot reaches the ground closer to the body. This is how elite walkers do.

Footwork

1. To increase speed, walk heel to toe and not flatfooted.
2. Touch the ground with your heel
3. Roll the foot forward over the center of your foot.
4. Push off using your toes.

Hips

1. Rotate your hips backward and forward as you walk.
2. Your waist should twist. Because of the hip rotation, racewalkers may look funny, but limited hip movement reduces your speed.

Torso

1. Your torso should be always upright. Leaning back or forward will slow you down.

Arm Work

1. Your elbows should always be at 90 degrees.
2. Keep your hands relaxed.
3. Swing your arms back and forward and keep them near to your body. To maintain efficiency, your hands should not cross the midline of your body.
4. To increase your speed, speed up your arm swing and your legs will follow. This is very effective.

Head, Shoulders and Neck

1. Keep your neck and shoulders relaxed. Your head should be upright. Your eyes should look forward.

Variants of Walking

Scrambling

Scrambling is a process of ascending a hill or mountain that involves the use of both hands, due to the steepness of the terrain. This requires a slow and careful form of walking and an occasional short, easy rock climbing. Some scrambling can be done on narrow exposed ridges which require more attention to balance than in normal walking.

Snow Shoeing

A snow shoe is footwear used for walking in the snow. It works by distributing the weight of the individual over a bigger area so that the individuals foot does not sink into the snow completely, a quality known as "flotation". Snowshoers believe that if you can walk, you can snowshoe. This could be true in optimal situations, but snowshoeing appropriately needs some slight changes to walking. The method of walking is to slightly lift the shoes and slide the inner edges over each other, thus preventing the fatiguing and unnatural straddle gait that would be necessary. A snowshoer should be willing to roll his feet a little bit as well. An exaggerated stride works best when starting, especially with traditional or larger shoes.

Nordic Walking

It is a physical sport and activity, which is carried out with specially manufactured walking poles just like ski poles. Nordic walking which is also called pole walking involves force to the poles with every stride. Nordic walkers make use of their entire body and get fitness building stimulation which is not seen in normal walking for the lats, shoulder, spinal, triceps, abdominals, biceps and other core muscles that may lead in increase heart rate at a given speed. Nordic walking can produce up to 46% increase in energy consumption, as compared to walking without poles.

Power Walking

This is also called as speed walking. It is an act of walking with a speed at the higher end of the natural range for walking gait, normally 4.5 to 5.5 mph. In order to classify as power walking as opposed to running or jogging, at least one foot should touch the ground all the times.

Racewalking

This is a long-distance athletic type of walking. Although it is a foot race, it differs from running in that one foot should touch the ground all the time. Stride length is reduced, to achieve the required speed, racewalkers should have cadence rates similar to what an Olympic 800 meter runners do.

Is Walking a Form of Workout?

You may be amazed to learn that brisk walking can be as challenging as jogging. Here are the reasons why. Each time you walk at speeds faster than 3.1 mph, it naturally increases your stride length (you don't actually want it for efficiency but it happens inevitably). Lengthening your stride is ineffective because it needs additional energy to move your legs forward, which also requires more torso and arm movement, which results to increased hip and torso rotation, which leads to higher aerobic demands and more calorie-burning. This has been proven in the laboratory. The study shows that at optimum levels of exertion, oxygen consumption is only less for racewalkers as compared to runners, and at moderate-intense level of exercise or submaximal, oxygen consumption levels between runners and race walkers are almost the same. The racewalkers can reach speeds up to 9 mph.

The Types of Foot Strike and What are the Biomechanics

The term used to describe the time your foot reaches the ground when you are walking is foot strike. Your heel should land first (heel strike), then by midfoot strike and followed by leveling of the arch to absorb impact, then the front of your foot strike, and then the push-off to the next stride is the normal biomechanics of foot strike. Soft heel strikes with a smooth gait pattern and some leveling of the arch will lessen the impact on the foot and will result in less stress on joints as high up as the hip. There are 3 types of foot strike.

1. Pronated foot strike. The term pronation is used to describe once your arch levels on foot strike and causes your foot to roll in, or invert. Too much pronation could be the reason for your leg and ankle to twist and can result in shin splints, stress fractures and lower-extremity injuries. If the inner edges of your footwear wear out, you are a pronator.

2. Supinated foot strike. The term used to describe high arches that don't level is supination. This could be a major concern because in case your arch does not level and your foot does not roll in, then you will not have shock absorption on foot strike. Too much supination can result in ankle sprains, plantar fasciitis, iliotibial band syndrome and Achilles tendinitis. If the outer edges of your shoes wear out, then you are a supinator.

3. Neutral foot strike. This is the term used to describe the efficient amount of leveling of the arch. This

provides lots shock absorption and good amount of energy for you to have a powerful push-off.

Walking Into a Healthy Life

Medical studies prove that regular exercise is good for health, but many of these studies combine various types of exercise together to investigate how the overall physical activity influences health. It is an essential research, but it does not necessarily prove that walking is beneficial.

Over 2400 years ago, Hippocrates stated, "Walking is man's best medicine." To determine if there is truth to what he said, scientists from University College London carried out a meta-analysis of research published between 1970 and 2007 in English-language journals. After examining the 4295 articles, they picked 18 studies that met their high standards for quality. These studies examined 459,833 participants who were not suffering from any cardiovascular disease when the study started. Each of the studies gathered information about the participants' walking practices together with details about cardiovascular risk factors, such as smoking, alcohol use and age and in some cases, additional health information as well. The participants were traced for an average of 11.3 years, during which cardiovascular diseases, such as angina, coronary artery bypass surgery, stroke, heart attack, angioplasty and heart failure and deaths were recorded.

The study makes a strong case for walking. The study shows that walking reduced the danger of having cardiovascular events by 31% and it lowered the risk of dying during the study period by 32%. These benefits were noticed in both men and women. Protection was obvious even at short distance per week and at a pace as casual as around 2 miles per hour. The individuals who walked at a faster rate, who walked longer distances, or both can have the best protection.

This meta-analysis contains reports from 7 countries on 3 continents. On the possibility of being chauvinistic, here is a short summary of three Harvard studies of walking and heart health:

- Out of 10,269 male graduates of Harvard College, walking 9 miles a week was associated with a 22% lower death rate.
- Out of 72,488 female nurses, walking 3 hours a week was associated with a 35% lower risk of cardiac death and heart attack and a 34% lower risk of stroke.
- Out of 44,452 male health experts, walking 30 mins a day was associated with an 18% lower risk of coronary artery disease.

Extra Steps

All eighteen studies in this 2008 British meta-analysis are observational analysis. As such, each study started with a defined group of volunteers free from any diseases known as cohort and then monitored them over a period of time that averaged 11.3 years to determine if those who walked enjoyed a reduced risk of having heart disease and a lower rate of death. The outcomes all provide a recommendation for walking, but randomized clinical trials are more conclusive than observational studies. However, one clinical trial of walking adds more weight to the other research. A ten year study of 229 postmenopausal women assigned randomly to walk at least one mile a day or to carry out their normal activities. When the trial ended, the walkers enjoyed an 82% reduced risk of cardiovascular disease.

All 459,833 who joined the meta-analysis were free from heart disease when they enrolled in the studies. If you already have heart disease, you can still get rehabilitated by walking. A study of 48 trials in 8946 patients showed that exercising moderately – generally walking or getting into stationary bicycle for 30 mins 3x a week, shows 26% reduction of having heart disease and a 20% reduction in overall death rate.

The Power of Walking

The cardiovascular benefits of walking are biologically reasonable. Like other types of regular workouts, walking improves heart risk factors like blood pressure, cholesterol, obesity, diabetes, vascular inflammation and stiffness and mental stress. And if heart protection and a reduced death rate are not enough to convince you to get moving, consider that walking together with exercise programs also help protect against depression, dementia, colon cancer, peripheral artery disease and even erectile dysfunction.

Chapter 2 – Six Scientific Facts About Walking

In Chapter 1, people were made to understand the health benefits of walking in nature. Shinrin-yoku or forest bathing, is a standard preventive cure in Japan. But at present, science has started to keep up, and an increasing body of research is showing the concrete mental and physical health benefits that walking provides. Some of these benefits will surprise even those long time walkers.

1. Helps You Cope at Work

Forget gulping caffeine, secretively checking Facebook and unwisely throwing your boss-directed anger on co-workers after several post-work drinks – the best way to deal with stress and pressure of salary slavery is by loving nature. A study funded by the ESRC or Economic and Social Research Council enumerates the benefits of the great outdoors by measuring responses to stress after and during viewing nature in both real and simulated environments.

The study proves that by looking at the slides of nature scenes one can improve recovery from a stressful task, as the scenes of built-up areas have the opposite result. Another study showed that a walk in the park with green environment at lunch time resulted in better sleep the following night, and after 8 weeks it resulted in the reduction of blood pressure and stress. If you can get that from a simple walk at the park during lunch time, just imagine if you do it regularly and during the weekends.

2. Walking is Sometimes Better than Running

People believe that running is the epitome of healthy living. What's healthier than jogging purposefully along with your trainers and bright clothes while listening with some inspiring music through headphones?

According to one research done by the Lawrence Berkeley National Laboratory in California, walking briskly regularly can reduce the risk of heart disease and is more effective compared to running. The study involved researchers comparing data from previous studies of 15,045 walkers and 33,060 runners over a period of 6 years. They discovered that for the same amount of energy utilized walkers experienced more health benefits as compared to runners, with the risk of cardio disease, blood pressure and cholesterol lowered by almost twice as much as running in some cases.

Of course, the outcomes had to involve the same amount of energy used. So since running utilizes around 2 ½ times the energy of walking, you have to spend 2 ½ times longer doing it. And another study shows that running is very effective in losing weight, while walking and running has the same effect on the risk of first time diabetes – both reducing it by around 12%.

Therefore, you can benefit both from walking and running – but walking could be better than you actually know.

3. It Helps You Concentrate

Just like your body, your brain gets exhausted. It is generally a muscle with thoughts, and just like other muscles it suffers from fatigue.

The strains and stresses of urban living, constant noise, and several other factors competing for your attention at one time intensify what is known as brain fatigue – when you are distracted, you become absent minded and have the attention distracted by other things.

People know that walking through green areas has a beneficial, calming effect on the mind, but a study in Scotland made use of technology to prove it. Brain scanning, lightweight devices were placed on the heads of twelve individuals who were then instructed to walk through Edinburgh. The study showed that while busy, congested areas induced irritation and frustration in the participants, parkland and green areas make the brain become calmer and more meditative. Naturally, this calmer condition helps with brain fatigue. A lecturer from Heriot-Watt's School of the Built Environment oversaw the study and told New York Times that natural environment engage our brain, the sort of engagement does not require a lot of effort. In psychology, it is known as involuntary attention. It holds the person's attention at the same you get to reflect on what you see.

4. It Cures Your Brain

Studies such as the one mentioned above may provide scientific evidence to back up something most people already are aware of, but they point the way to a much better understanding of precisely how nature works to enhance and soothe our mental condition.

Urban areas are mentally demanding locations to be – dodging vehicles, weaving through pedestrians, cramming on the trains, fielding phone calls and staring at screens require the brain to be continuously engaged, leaving a small area for meditating and reflecting.

By contrast, researchers have claimed the fascinating sights and sounds of nature evoke. Instead of overwhelming it with the energy weakening hard stimuli of urban environments, natural environments gently engage the brain while letting it enough space to ponder in the background on life's complexities and quandaries. In short, it allows your mind off the hook for sometime, going for a walk lets your brain to roam together with your body.

5. It Makes You More Creative

Nietzsche wrote, "all truly great thoughts are conceived by walking." This feeling is echoed by others. Henry Thoreau wrote, "Methinks the time my legs start to move, my thoughts start to flow."

Freedom to think is an important part of the creative process, so it follows that the mental unshackling walking provides boost the creativity of an individual. Scientists agree on this. Dr. Sowden fo the School of Psychology at the University of Surrey states that walking has been very effective in improving the ability to shift between modes of thought, and to enhance the memory, attention and recovery from the mental fatigue, all of which are essential for thinking creatively. Also, according to him walking exposes people to the continuous flux of a changing environment giving people an endless array of unique and new experiences, which combine with the person's past memories may, through serendipity alone trigger new associations and provide new ideas. Although it must be made mention that at some point, you need to stop walking and carry out some actual task.

6. It Can Cure Depression

A study done by the University of Stirling on 341 individuals proved that brisk walking was an effective intervention for depression and has the same effect as compared to other vigorous types of workout. The Mental Health Charity Mind carries out their own research to back up this study. It's chief executive, Paul Farmer, told the BBC. Working out with others may have a better effect, since it provides an opportunity to strengthen social networks, discuss your problems with others or just laugh and have a break form work and family. So it is best if you ask your friends to join you.

The benefits of physical exercise mostly on treating mental conditions are well documented. Based on one study, physical activities are very effective as compared to medication in curing depression.

Mental Benefits of Walking

As mentioned in Chapter 1, walking can lower blood pressure, decrease the risk of stroke and having other cardio disease, lessen joint pressure and help maintain your weight. It also helps you decrease stress, improves memory and helps you sleep better at night. While walking boasts several physical benefits, it can also provide the brain mental boosts.

Here are some of the mental benefits of walking:

Slows Down Mental Decline

A study involving 6000 women, from 65 years old and above, was carried out by scientists at the University of California, San Francisco, discovered that age-related memory decline was lower in women who walked more. The women walking 2.5 miles everyday had a 17% decline in memory, as opposed to a 25% decline in women who walked less than ½ mile per week.

Scientists from the University of Pittsburgh performed the study on the latest brain scans of the participants. The average age of the participants was 78 years old. The other study was carried out four years ago, checking for signs and symptoms of cognitive problem. After 4 yours the result is around 40% of the group developed signs of memory impairment or dementia.

However, those who have produced more steps were half as likely to have these mental issues. As for the target amount of steps, when it comes to solving the mental deterioration, the study suggests that you should walk around 72 blocks every week. The study showed that making more steps, although good for the body, did not provide more cognitive benefits.

This study backs up past research which shows that regular workout can decrease the danger of developing Alzheimer's.

If regular workout in midlife could improve brain health and memory and thinking in later life, it would be another reason to do regular workouts in individuals of all ages.

Lowers the Risk of Alzheimer

A study done at the University of Virginia Health System in Charlottesville found that men between 71 yrs old and 93 yrs old who walked more than a quarter of a mile each day had half the incidence of Alzheimer's disease and dementia, as compared to those who walked less.

Walking 5 miles every week may keep your brain protective and slow cognitive decline in individuals with MCI or mild cognitive impairment and Alzheimer's disease, said researchers at a conference in Chicago of medical imaging professionals, they likewise found that walking 6 miles a week have the same result for healthy individuals.

Dr. Cyrus Raji, from the University of Pittsburgh in Pennsylvania presented the results of a study where he and his team analyzed changes in brain volume among adults with different level of cognitive impairment, including some suffering from Alzheimer's and also healthy individuals, whose weekly physical activity had been observed in a heart study over the past ten years.

According to Dr. Raji, the study found out that 5 miles per week protects the structure of the brain over ten years in individuals with MCI and Alzheimer's, particularly in areas of the brain's important memory and learning centers. These individuals also had a slower decline in memory loss for the past 5 years.

Mild Cognitive Impairment, is where an individual has more concerns with thinking and memory skills than his typical age, but it is not as serious as that found in Alzheimer's disease. Around 50% of individuals diagnosed with Mild Cognitive Impairment progress to Alzheimer's disease.

The numbers of Americans with Alzheimer's and MCI is increasing significantly over the next decade, based on present population trends.

Alzheimer's disease is incurable, which is why researchers such as Raji and his team are eager to find ways to improve the symptoms and slow down the progression of the disease in individuals whose memory and thinking are already displaying signs of deterioration.

Raji and his team recruited participants from the Cardiovascular Health Study, which is still continuing and has been gathering data for twenty years, and study the connection between their brain structure and physical activity.

The study involved 426 participants, composed of 127 cognitively impaired individuals of ages 81 years old, and 299 healthy individuals of ages 78 years old. Of the cognitively impaired individuals who jointed this study, 44 had Alzheimer's dementia and 83 had MCI.

The study data enabled the researchers to determine how far participants walked in a week. Then ten years later they carried out 3D MRI scans of their brains to check for any changes in brain volume.

Volume is an important sign for the brain. When it decreases, it means that the cells are dying. But if it remains higher, brain health is being maintained. Also, the participants completed the MMSE or the mini-mental state exam, which let the researchers track cognitive decline over 5 years.

Raji and his team then correlated physical activity levels with MMSE and MRI results and adjusted the results to remove any influence due to variations in gender, head size, body mass, age, education and other possible cofounders like white matter hyperintensities, believed to be a kind of brain cell damage associated with vascular risk factors of dementia. The primary result showed that across the board, the more workout participants took, the higher their brain volume.

During their session abstract, the researchers noted that greater physical activity was associated with greater volumes of occipital, hippocampal, frontal, temporal and entorhinal regions 9 years later.

For participants with cognitive problem, waking for at least fifty eight city blocks, or five miles, every week, were associated with protection of brain volume and gradual decline in cognitive.

For healthy contributors, walking at least 72 city blocks, or 6 miles every week was enough to maintain the brain volume and reduce significantly the risk of cognitive decline.

The researchers noted that walking more than this threshold level did not seem to preserve any more brain volume.

The outcomes showed that more than 5 years, for the cognitively impaired participants who was not able to attain the threshold level of activity, the scores on the MMSE cognitive test decline by 5 points on average, as compared to only 1 point on average for those who did meet the physical activity required. According to Raji Alzheimer is a distressing illness, and unfortunately, walking will not cure the disease. But, it can help your brain repel the disease and slow down memory loss.

The National Institute on Aging estimates that between 2.4 and 5.1 million American's are suffering from Alzheimer's disease, irreversible, progressive and devastating brain disease that slowly destroys thinking and memory, in advanced stage, individuals lose the capability to carry on a respond and conversation to their environment.

Alzheimer's is the 6th leading cause of death in the US, where it accounts for the 50 to 70% of dementia cases. Although most people who get the disease are usually aged 65 and over, around one in twenty cases are early onset, affecting individuals in their 40s and 50s.

Improves Sleep

A study from the Fred Hutchinson Cancer Research Center in Seattle found that women, from ages 50 years old to 75 years old, who completed a one-hour morning walks, were more likely to solve insomnia as compared to women who didn't walk.

It may look like the fact that walking improves sleep for many people, including insomniacs, is just common sense. Present studies support the commonsense view that walking and other workout improves sleep. Research also proves that individuals who workouts most of the time take less time to fall asleep as compared to individuals who don't.

And walking can help you spend a lot of time in deeper stages of sleep. This is vital because waking up is more common during the lighter part of sleep.

Timing is also very important. A brisk walk before going to sleep may cause you some issues with sleep. If you have been walking before going to sleep and have trouble falling or staying asleep, or even have problems with insomnia, do your walk earlier in the day. Try walking in the afternoon for many weeks to see what happens.

There is some indication that exercise encourages sleep by heating the brain and body. This hypothesis is dependable with evidence that even body heating in a hot tub or sauna for instance, can increase slow-wave sleep.

Lightens Mood

It was posted in the British Journal of Sports Medicine the research that walking thirty minutes a day can boost the moods in a depressed patient faster as compared to antidepressants. It's because walking releases endorphins a natural pain killing to the body – one of the emotional benefits of working out. A study conducted at the California State University, Long Beach, showed that the more steps people make during the day, the better their moods.

Aside from these mental benefits of walking, it is also a form of meditation. A stroll outside can help eliminate a bad day as you focus on what you see around you. Some of the successful race-walking athlete started with a simple walk in the park. Carolyn S. Kortge started walking in the 80's and joined the first race-walking competition in the 90's, who eventually becomes the USA Track and Field Association silver and bronze race-walking medalist. She was diagnosed with osteoarthritis in 2004, but continues to ignore the pain in her knees and hands by walking every day.

Chapter 3 – Why Walk Your Way to Weight Loss?

Walking is amazingly one of the easiest, cheapest, and safest ways for you and everyone else to get up and start exercising. Health experts all agree that a 30-minute, moderate physical activity on most days in a week is a must, and walking is one of the best examples around. There have been so many reported health benefits of walking, like reducing the risks for certain medical conditions (heart disease and high blood pressure as discussed in Chapter 1), reducing depression, making us much happier and livelier instead, helping us all to sleep better at night (which is simply what everyone wants these days), and of course WEIGHT LOSS. Better yet, think of walking as an all-in-one package program with all the amazing health benefits. Nothing could be better than this.

The same health experts also agree on the fact that engaging in physical activities regularly is your strong foundation for good health and wellbeing, and walking happens to be the easiest and cheapest way to become physically active. Simply grab a good pair of shoes and you are all set to brisk walk (by the way, brisk walking is highly considered an ideal moderate-level physical activity) your way to weight loss and staying thin forever. Walking burns off all those unwanted fats dangling in our bellies so they could be converted into fuel our body needs.

You can even customize your brisk walking to the way you seem fit. Divide your 30-minute walking sessions into much shorter periods of 10-minute walks each. You can make things more interesting by opting for the stairs instead of the boring (and sometimes monotonous) elevator ride, or get off your bus at a stop, or two, from your destination. Hey, you now have a reason to park your car at the far end of the lot.

And once you are already fully engaged in your 30-minute-a-day moderate physical activity, you can get more from the package simply by "doing more." You can engage in moderate-level activities for longer periods (those that you can tolerate), or start engaging in more vigorous activities. Whatever the case is, walking your way to weight loss is the foundation needed.

And There Are More Benefits

As already mentioned walking your way to weight loss is like getting a good package deal because of the numerous health benefits to be had, and none of the setbacks and risks that frequently follows other physical activities. Aside from reducing the risks of dying from stroke or heart disease, walking also lowers your risks to developing diabetes, colon cancer, and other cancer types, like breast cancer. And unlike jogging, which is more physical, walking protects against the usual injuries, like tripping and falling down, and against bone fractures for older adults. Walking also increases the calorie that your body would use on a daily basis. This helps much in controlling weight. Then there's also fact that walking eases the pain and joint swelling caused by arthritis.

Walking helps you feel light. If you are under heavy stress, walk some miles and all those anxieties and depression will go away. It grants you an opportunity to actively socialize with family and friends. It'll also improve your self-esteem and love life all the way, that is if you start walking on a regular basis.

Chapter 4 – Before Starting Your Walking Program

Since walking has given us so many health benefits, with weight loss the number one item in the list, it is not surprising at all that many have started exploiting its flexibility and integrating walking into their daily and busy lives. And if you want to start a walking program right away, satisfy yourself first with these questions. If you happen to answer "yes" to these, you better talk to your healthcare provider first before making that first step.

- Have you been ever told that you are having heart trouble, asthma, or diabetes?
- Are you over 50 years old, and not really used to doing physical activities?
- Whenever you are physically active, do you experience chest, shoulders, neck, or arms pain?
- Are you feeling extremely breathless after your physical activities?
- Do you feel like fainting on a frequent basis, or have dizzying spell sessions?
- Do you have joint or bone problems (arthritis)?
- Do you smoke?
- Are you pregnant?
- Are you suffering from certain health problems or physical reasons that could keep you from launching your walking program?

Walking Your Way to Weight Loss

Now that you've gotten past those questions, it's time to move forward. You need not have a gym membership to start this very effective exercise as well. As walking is considered the exercise of choice to most dieters and virtually anyone looking for surefire ways to bring their weight down to healthier levels, you can readily walk on virtually everywhere that you see fit (you can do some fun walks around the block or mall for example).

Walking is a particular exercise that is gentle on joints, and it can burn for you a number of calories. Going on flat terrain, your 30-minute brisk walks could chew up seventy-five to a hundred calories. Conquer some hills and you'll be burning up to 250 calories. This may be a challenge, but what you get from it is very rewarding.

Finding Good Shoes

As already mentioned previously, you only need some comfortable walking shoes to launch your walking program. While you won't be having a hard time looking for a good pair, comfort matters the most. If you feel good wearing one, it's because your choice of shoes provides you with enough support. Aside from the proper support, your walking should also feature good arch support, thick flexible soles to cushion the feet (it also acts as a good shock absorber), and a firm heel. If you are walking on a frequent basis, you may want to purchase new shoes on a regular basis. It would also be smart to consult with a podiatrist regarding effective walking shoes.

When shopping for walking shoes and other useful equipment, you have to:

1. Wear the socks that you are going to use for your walking. This way you'll get the most comfortable fit there is.
2. You also have to try on both shoes. Putting on one and deciding this is perfect for you is not the way to find really comfortable shoes.
3. Always allow for an extra room. Note that your feet normally swells as you walk around, it only makes sense to go for pairs with a thumb's width between the shoe and your longest toe.
4. You should also make sure that the heel wouldn't slip up as you walk, or else you'll end up with blisters at the end of the day.
5. During winter, always wear a firm cap for extra warmth. Walking during winter is no good if you are not comfortable with the weather. Come summertime, you could stay cool by wearing a visor, or a baseball cap.
6. Wear garments that discourage inner-thigh chafing (this can be very uncomfortable and painful when walking), such as spandex shorts or tights. You'll feel much comfortable walking using clothes that keep you dry. Buy synthetic fabrics designed to absorb sweat, removing it away from your skin.

Determine the Type of Foot You Have

In order to choose the right shoes, you should determine first the type of foot you have. As mentioned in Chapter 1, there are two types of foot, the supinate and the pronate. If you don't know what type of food you have, you can ask a salesperson from a trusted shoe store to check your gait and foot strike, or you can ask your doctor or podiatrist to do this. In determining the type of foot you have, you can do the wet test at home. To do this, simply wet your bare foot and then step on a piece of paper or other area that will display your footprint. To do this, you need to stand normally with slight pressure toward the front of your foot. If most of your foot hits the floor, then you are a pronator, if less of your foot hits the ground then you are a supinator, and for neutral, the footprint is somewhere between supination and pronation.

What Type of Footwear to Purchase?

One of the advantages of walking is that it doesn't require lots of fancy tools and equipment, but footwear can make a difference. There are lots of athletic shoe types to pick from. So for walking, you need walking shoes. This type of footwear basically has heels and toes that are rounded up to lessen the impact on heel strike and boost energy during push-off. Here are guidelines on how to decide what type of walking footwear to purchase based on your foot strike and foot type.

If you have flat feet and pronate, stay away from shoes with excessive cushioning since they lack motion control and stability. Footwear that feels as soft as the bedroom slippers, usually lack support, or are excessively bouncy are not the best choice for over-pronators. This type of shoes can decrease pressure up to 33%. Superfeet and Powerfeet full-length insoles are the perfect choices and can be purchased online.

For supinate individuals and have high arches, choose cushioned footwear that does not restrict motion. If you have arches and supinate, your foot doesn't shock absorb, and too much control and stability in the shoe will lessen shock absorption even more.

For those with neutral foot, you can wear any kind of shoe that feels comfortable. Your foot strike is efficient with a good amount of arch support and shock absorption.

The Shoe Shopping Basics

Here are tips that every person should follow when purchasing walking shoes:

1. The sole of the walking shoe should be flexible having more bend in the toe as compared to the running shoe. The possibility of having blisters is high if the shoe is too stiff. It is important that you can twist and bend the toe area of your walking shoe.
2. Breathable shoes are more comfy. Mesh fabrics are much better that leather and they are lighter, too.
3. Shoes should make you feel comfortable right away – there is no breaking in period. Do not choose shoes if you can feel the stitching or seams. This may result to calluses, blisters or other foot problems.
4. Feet are bigger during the day so purchase your walking shoes at the end of the day when your foot is at its largest.
5. Use socks you usually use when walking. Socks made of synthetic materials like polypropylene or other synthetics are better as compared to cotton since they don't compress, they wick moisture away from foot,

the heel is padded, and dry quickly.
6. Allow ½ inch between the end of your longest toe and the shoe's end, with enough room for your toes to wiggle.
7. The shoes should be as wide as possible across the forefoot without heel slippage. To get the right fit, experiment with the lacing.
8. Before buying the shoes, always try on both shoes. Purchase the larger size if one foot is bigger than the other.
9. Replace your walking shoes if you feel they no longer support your feet. You will know your present shoe is worn down if use them when purchasing a new pair. You can feel the difference after fitting the new pair.
10. Look for a reputable shoe store in your area.

How to Start Walking to Lose Weight?

For starters who are concerned about their ability or motivation to walk far, experts suggest that you start with "five minutes out, five minutes back" program. You walk out for 5 minutes, turn around and walk back. If you feel 5 minutes' walk is not enough, you can start with ten minutes out, ten minutes back. Increase 2 or 3 minutes per week and before you know it you are doing 30 minutes a day. It sounds very simple, but this is a realistic and is an achievable way to get you started, and if you follow it, you will be walking longer before you know it.

If you want to increase your speed, consider power-walking. Begin with your normal walking speed for 5 to 10 minutes as a warm-up and then check your skill at power-walking. You will be surprised how tiring power-walking can be, so begin with ten to fifteen minutes and finish up your thirty minutes with your normal walking pace so you will not overdo it.

Interval Training

Upon reaching the baseline of thirty minutes of power-walking, you can increase your speed even more by training with intervals. Setting up work to active rest ratios refers to intervals, to push your body and improve your cardiorespiratory health. Here is an example of how to perform intervals.

For 3 minutes, walk at your normal speed, then

1. Increase the speed for one minute, then
2. Walk again with your normal speed for another 3 minutes, then
3. Do this again 1:3 intervals cycling to complete your workout.
4. As you continue with your walking increase the work and reduce the active rest.

Here is an example of an interval training exercise for someone who walks for thirty minutes at 3.5 mph.

1. For ten minutes, walk at 3.5 mph, then
2. Add more speed to 3.8 mph for 1 minute, then
3. Walk again for 3 mins at 3.5 mph, then
4. Walk again at 3.8 mph, and so on till you reach your limit.
5. Increase the working part to ½ minutes and reduce the active rest to 2 ½ minutes as you get fit (you walk faster, your cardio does not pump hard, and you

breathe much easier).

Your health will improve significantly after 6 to 8 weeks if you continue with kind of training. After 1 or 2 sessions, you may notice more endurance.

Chapter 5 – Your Walking Form

While walking, wherever you may be, comes naturally, and you're smart enough to follow that technique you already honed since back in your toddler days, these tips should help you stay comfortable so your walking becomes effective and your weight loss goal is realized. Such disciplines should also help maximize your burn.

1. While walking, learn to stand straight. Think of a string on the top portion of your head that pulls you up all the time. Let it pull you up straight while walking. Relax your shoulders all the way.
2. Always look what's ahead of you. This means keeping your neck straight and head up high to prevent straining your shoulders and neck. If you want to look down, look using your eyes, and not your head.
3. Always move those arms while walking. This completes the process of having all your muscles in your body works while walking. Besides, you'll get to burn off 15% more of those calories. Bend the elbows and let the arms swing at your sides naturally.
4. Carrying weights are a no-no. Some folks think that getting in that extra exercise in their walking programs can be achieved by toting light dumbbells, but this is wrong according to fitness-walking experts. It's a risky business as well; the weights will put you off-balance while walking. It also strains your legs and back at the same time.
5. Learn how to activate your abs while walking. As you brace your core (pull your belly button inwards

toward the spine) you encourage good posture automatically.

6. Squeeze the glutes. Remember that your backside normally propels you forward as you walk. To get the most of your walking activities, and that you can go on faster and longer as well, learn to squeeze your glutes tight.

7. Always choose a safe place where you could walk unimpeded. It would also be great if walk with a partner or a group. Your walking partners should be in-sync with you – all of you could walk together at the same speed and time. Sync your walking schedule with theirs.

8. Do not feel lazy in the ritualistic light stretching sessions after you had your warm-ups and cool-downs.

9. As already mentioned, schedule your walking activities 3 times a week at the least. And as you progress by, try to increase the minutes in your walks to better your chances at weight loss. If you can only afford to walk less than 3 times in a week, then you may need time to adjust things before attempting to increase the frequency and pace of your walks.

10. As you start your walking program, it would be smart to start gradually to prevent sore and stiff joints and muscles. Take it slowly. This is where you warm up walks and stretching come in real handy. Besides, you could start increasing your intensity as the weeks pass by. You could then walk faster, go farther, and walk for much longer periods.

11. Before you start your walking program, you must

already have set your goals and rewards. This helps your weight loss effort big time.

Stretching

It all starts with warming up your muscles through 5-minute easy walks before and after your main walking sessions. The following stretches should help make your muscles flexible. Never hold or bounce your breath as you stretch. Perform slow movements; stretch as far as it would be comfortable for you.

- The Side Reach – This is achieved by reaching an arm over the head and onto the side. Keep the hips steady, shoulders straight on the sides. Hold for about 10 seconds. Repeat it to the other side afterwards.
- The Wall Push – to start, lean on the wall with your hands and your feet 3 to 4 feet away from the wall. Bend a knee afterwards pointing to the wall. While doing this, your back leg must be kept straight, foot flat with the toes pointing straight ahead. Hold this position for 10 seconds before repeating the procedure with your other leg.
- The Leg Curl – This exercise tells you to pull your foot up into your buttocks using your hand while standing straight all the while. Point the knee to the ground as well. Hold for 10 seconds and repeat using your other foot.
- The knee Pull – To do this, you have to lean against a wall, with your head, feet and hips lined up straight. Pull a knee all the way to your chest and hold it for 10 seconds before repeating it again using the other leg.

- The Hamstring Exercise – This will require you to sit on hard surface to facilitate your left leg stretching outwards with the toes pointing up. Plant your right foot firmly on the floor. With your back straightened, you'll feel a stretch somewhere on your thigh's back. Hold onto this position for 10 seconds and repeat with the other leg. If you have yet to feel that stretch, try leaning forward until you get the stretch.

Chapter 6 – Walking Your Way Towards Weight Loss

This is it. You are now ready to start walking and trimming your weight off one at a time. You may not believe it now, but you can target 10 pounds off with your walking so long as you have the will, motivation, and dedication to see it through. You can walk it all off, drop 10 pounds and flatten your belly in just as little as a month.

Such target is best achieved with "fast-paced" walking. And when you incorporate your brisk walks with healthy eating, you'll surely find your way to effective weight loss. This simple program introduces a very big impact on your health. If your daily strolls have yet to make you lean or skinny however, it could be that speed is your problem. Believe it or not, many of us are simply contented to be more like window shoppers than the ideal "power walker" who walks with a real purpose. Fortunately, the goal here is nothing like what you see in walkathons; you simply need to walk at challenging paces.

Studies have proven how women who regularly performs 3 short 30-minute walks at high intensity balanced with two moderate-paced recovery walks all in one week would shed off abdominal fat six times more than those who simply stroll along 5 days in a week. This is true despite how both groups of women burn down the same number of calories.

The power walkers are also known to drop 4 times of their total body fat than the other walkers. Scientists have connected how the intensity of the walking exercise and those fat-burning hormones work together and determined how such relationship bring about effective weight loss. This means that if you walk at a challenging pace, you would release more of the fat-burning hormones. The exciting part of it all is that those deep abdominal fats are usually the first to go.

Another happy fact we ought to know about is that our fast-paced walking is still much easier on our joints than when running. When you walk one foot always stay on the ground. It's a different story when it comes to running though, as you experience a float stage – your body is being lifted into the air. And once you come down your body is subjected to the eventual impact.

This is why walking will always be the smart fitness plan in the long term. And it does not skimp on its own ability to burn fat, lose weight, and keep you lean and skinny. To achieve this, you must learn the proper walking mechanics aside from your walking form that has already been tackled here.

The Amount of Calories You Can Lose By Walking

A 150-lb man can burn 100 calories per mile. A 200-lb man burns 133 calories per mile. A 250-lb man burns 166 calories per mile. The amount of calories you burn from running or walking a mile are virtually the same. You only get there faster if you run.

What is a Good Average Walking Pace?

- A good average walking pace is three to four miles per hour and depends on the length of your leg and how fast you can move your legs.

- You may require starting at a slow speed if you are out of shape, but you will increase faster if you walk regularly.
- It gets tricky once you surpass 4 mph because you are confused if you should run or walk. Proper speed-walking technique will help at a faster pace.
- Outdoor walking and treadmill provide the same benefits. Set the elevation to 1% to simulate outdoor walking.

The Amount of Walking You Need To Do

Experts recommend these two walking workouts:

1. The Surgeon General suggests thirty minutes or more of "total" moderate intensity physical activity on 5 or more days per week to improve fitness and health. "Total" means you can divide it into shorter bouts within the day, and moderate intensity means you slightly out of breath and feels warm when you perform it.

Here are some ways on how to incorporate walking into your daily routine and accumulate thirty minutes. Think about your daily activities and how you can increase walking.

- Get off the bus before reaching your destination.
- Park your vehicle farther from your destination
- Take a walk at lunch rather than having your food delivered.

- Walk for errands rather than driving short distances.
- Dispose your riding lawnmower

Make sure that your walking shoes are handy. You can take a quick ten minute stress reducing walks during your break time, so make sure that you leave a pair of walking shoes at your office.

2. The American College of Sports Medicine suggests twenty to sixty minutes of continuous activity, 3 to 5 times a week, at 60 to 90% of maximum heart rate, and 2 to 3 days of resistance raining.

Chapter 7 – Walk This Way, Walk That Way

To get things going, here's a detailed primer starting from tweaking the speed so you'll get the maximum burn to the gears you'll need in your walk. Think of these workouts and wisdom – together with healthy eating – as your guide to lose that targeted 10 pounds in just less a month. Remember, you can walk anywhere you want, anytime you want.

You're Speed

Your aim here should be to make sure your pace is right on point. For a maximized fat burn, go for a 30-minute intensified powerwalk for 3 days. You can complete all of them at once. You may also opt to break them down into spurts by having recovery strides (strolls) in between.

- Strolling – Imagine when you are window-shopping and the pace you are doing it. On a scale of 1 to 10, you could step it up to an 'intensity 4'. This should help you burn 238 calories in every hour.
- Brisk Walk – After that intensity 4 stroll, you can brisk walk it all up with an intensity 5, or maybe 6, on a 1-10 scale. At this pace you could burn a good 340 calories max in an hour.
- The Power Walk – Here, you'll be torching about 564 calories for every hour (at an approximately 4 to 5 mph pace). While moving at this serious speed, you'll have to utilize your arms when moving forward using longer strides. On the 1-10 scale, you should be giving it a 7 to 8 intensity effort to perform the power walk.

You can talk with your partner here, but only in spurts. And that is just normal.

Amp It All Up

This approach mixes regular walking workouts with the usual interval routines to assist you in reaching your 30-minute, 3-times-a-week power-walking quota. Condition yourself to walk on 3 separate days and then cross-train or rest in between. Should you cross-train (this can either be swimming or power yoga) you'll be doing your body a favor by helping it to recover. And if you follow a sound diet plan, your walking to weight loss effort will progress much faster than you anticipated it.

- The Tempo Combo – Here, you'll get to burn 220 calories by doing warm-ups (strolling for about 5 minutes), your main walking workout (maintaining the power-walk intensity for a good 30 minutes), and the cool down (an easy stroll that last for 5 minutes).
- The Long Interval Combo – This intensified walking program will make you burn 355 calories. Start by warming up with a 5-minute stroll, followed by an interval workout. Here, you'll have to maintain a hard-paced power-walk intensity (this should be on the 8 in the 1-10 scale) for a whole 5 minutes before recovering at a brisk pace for about a minute. This should give you good results after doing 6 intervals. Top it all off with a cool down stroll up to 5 minutes.
- The Short Interval Combo – Doing this will burn you up to 405 calories. And just like the other combos you start with a warm-up stroll for about 5 minutes, followed immediately by the interval workout (power

walk with a hard-paced intensity) for about 2 minutes. Recover afterwards with a brisk walking pace for a minute. Repeat this interval 15 times for maximum effect. Stroll for about 5 minutes to cool down.

Other Ways to Burn Fat Better While Walking

Assuming you are the impatient type, you can simply take it a notch higher and give yourself a bigger, yet achievable, challenge. Conquer hills. When you hit the hills around the neighborhood, or on your treadmill, you improve your body's burning of calories up to an astonishing 20%. And what we're talking about here is a 1 to 5 percent incline.

You can also go on adventure by going off-road. Head out to light but brisk hiking trails and you'll register 430 calories burned in just a single hour. Force your way into uneven terrain; this only forces you to work harder. It would be ideal if you could get this adventurous for once during your weekly power walks.

And while at it, swing your arms. Get your whole body involved for better weight loss. Bend your elbows at 90 degrees, fist and loose your hands away by swinging your arms in a wide arc. Keep your elbows close to your body to help you propel forward. This, at the same time, helps to build your upper-body strength, as well as increase the calories you burn up to a total of 10%.

It would also be ideal to aim for longer strides. Instead of walking more steps, try working on your stride length. Not only will you cover more ground, you'll also fry more of the fats.

Chapter 8 – More Smart Walking Ideas

Always consider that the more you walk about, the more calories you get to burn and the better you would feel about yourself as well. Fitness walking experts will always recommend the 30-minute moderate to intense walking on most days. If you think this is too much for you now, you could always try walking on shorter distances and work your way from there eventually.

Believe In the Power of Cross Training Through Variations Of Your Walking Workouts

People usually have this belief that they would walk for six miles every day using the same route and get good things from there. But the thing is you could always cut the workout time into half and still achieve the same results simply by changing how you walk. This is more practical and evenly effective.

If you make it a habit to do the same things on a regular basis, you can expect your body to adapt to it – enter the "conservative mode." This is part of how you maintain stasis. Your mind also adapts here by the way. Soon, you get the feeling that your walking workouts get boring, and that you are surprised to find out that you are not able to keep walking at the same vigorous pace as you had when you are fully motivated to walk your unnecessary weight off. Not only is momentum lost here; you also lose that "training effect."

If you can cycle and swim in between days of your walking workouts, then that would be great. Make things interesting.

Make your weight loss effort thru walking interesting to you, and you'll never get bored. Remember however, that walking is that ideal exercise you can always take with you wherever you go all your life. You can virtually walk just anywhere you wish, so long as it is comfortable and you are not invading other people's spaces. How your heart rate is conditioned depends on the various terrain that you conquer. And when you go indoors, you'll be using different muscles in various ways and in different resistance levels.

Care to use the treadmill at least once a week. On a separate day, you could walk your dog, or meet a friend on a casual stroll. Their effects may not be as dramatic as that of cross trainings, like cycling and switching to swimming, but it creates an ideal positive environment that brings fun and new perspectives to your walking effort as compare to trekking the same path for years.

Adding More Flavor With Intensity Bursts

Another school of thought that we are used to be that the longer you walk it out, the more likely it is that your body systematically goes on fat-burning mode. Then there's also the theory that after long workouts of up to 60 or 90 minutes, the human body again settles into "conserve mode. But the fact of the matter is that if you incorporate short intense bursts into your regular walking program, you'll enhance your fat-burning mode even after your workout, instead of going into conserve mode. And this is practically more efficient in every way.

As already detailed above, run-walk combos are your best bet. With an added interval workout filled with intense bursts for a few minutes and done twice a week, your chances of walking to weight loss will definitely get better. If you can add two serious 15 to 20 minute workout interval in every week complete with a longer, yet moderately-paced workout, then that should be a great stat for you. From here, you can add an additional walking workout that's long and very intense.

Try Walking With a Coach Three Times A Week

Or better yet, get his/her wisdom via cd/DVD. To change is really hard. It takes your will and a good direction. All of us need help. Everyone knows that effective training tools are vital, but the coaching component is imperative in achieving new levels of health fitness. A good walking coach could get you to places that you could not get on your own. He/She will bring out the best in you, giving you another clear perspective on what you want to accomplish with your walking activities.

Expect your coach to be there with you in every step of your progress and missteps. He/She is the best person to help your way from scratch all towards effective weight loss.

Even if you are already getting on with your intense powerwalks, you could listen to CDs loaded with coaching wisdom and accompanying workout music. This is designed to motivate and remind you of your potentials and everything you could accomplish given your dedication and training. It also reminds you how valuable your walking workout is to your weight loss goals. The whole coaching process helps you physically as well, this is achieved by helping you move your heart rate around and then changing your body's intensity levels while doing your powerwalks.

Walk to Live Better, Not Just to Lose Weight

This is a great principle to guide you by. Understand that at 30, your body normally starts to lose bone mass. You would find yourself exerting more effort in building and supporting your body than usual. This is the time where you want your balance to stay sharp and your joints strong, and you want the stress from daily work to just go away. But best of all there are other positive benefits to be had with walking. Not only would you get refreshed after every walking session, you feel so alive and happy, and such feelings get you addicted you'll be craving for more to offset your daily troubles at work. All these lead to a healthy life all the way as you age, and you know there's no better way to enjoy life onwards than living a healthy, sick-free life with family and friends.

Walking Towards Success? Change Your Mindset As Well

It's true that you need not bother changing and improving your body and wellbeing if you won't care to change your mindset about life as a whole. If you do, it will only be temporary, and it will just add up to your past failures. It is only normal that we humans condition ourselves to fail. We are sometimes conditioned ourselves to fail, convinced that we can't do it based probably on past dieting and weight loss experiences.

If you think hard about it, this is another important reason why you should incorporate intensity bursts and make things more interesting in jump starting your fat-burning machine. The faster you can achieve positive results, the better your belief will be that you'll attain success with your walking efforts. This is unarguably the fastest approach to change how your body and mind work together towards your weight loss goals. Many believe that the whole universe has what we're thinking, and that if we really wanted it or not. Our beliefs, thoughts, obsessions, and fears will always drive our actions. Settle down and focus on what you want to achieve, not on what you do not want.

And if you really want to lose weight in the best way possible, think clearly how much of the unnecessary weight you wanted to lose and what you would want to look and feel like afterwards. It's never all about hating how heavy you are right now. To steer you to the right direction, always picture yourself healthy and fit.

Chapter 9 - Using Pedometer in Walking to Shape Up and Slim Down

It has been discussed in the previous chapters how effective walking is in losing weight and burning fats. This chapter will discuss how a pedometer can help you to effectively lose weight through walking. Prevention's pedometer plan will get you off the couch, reduce your danger of having the disease, and help you lose weight.

A pedometer is a device that looks like a beeper, you can clip it in your waist and it only cost around $30. It is used traditionally by racewalkers to track the number of steps the walkers have made. The pedometer is one of the most powerful motivators you have ever encountered. Studies show that sedentary individuals who use pedometers and have a daily goal are more active all day and show improvements in fitness and body fat compared to individuals doing the more structured workout.

If you belong to the group who believe that only vigorous workout like jogging two miles – counts toward fitness, you need to think again. The study done about pedometer proves that increasing your daily activities – walking the dog and just getting up more often – can make a big difference. Thus, researches decided to give a pedometer program a try.

A group of overweight individuals was subjected in a walking pedometer program to lose weight. Based on the amount of steps they normally took, the group is divided into two. Those who were inactive had an objective of achieving 10,000 steps, while those who were active had an objective of achieving 18,000 steps. After eight weeks, they saw some changes in weight, cholesterol, fitness and body fat.

The Unknown Facts About Pedometer

This device is less expensive, easy to use and does not require an expert to use it. All you need to do is to snap it on and check it every now and then. There is no need for you to make time the way you have to plan for going to an aerobics class or visiting the gym. Hooking on a pedometer can become part of your daily activities. The greatest strength of the pedometer is its ability to motivate. You can park your car farther away from your destination, instead of using the elevator you can use the stairs. After doing this, you will discover that it does make a difference. After you take a walk, it is satisfying to discover your steps ticking away. It is like a pat on the back. It tells you to be more active. If you feel or see the pedometer on your waistband, you will be reminded to get moving, particularly if you have got a long way to go to hit your objective.

Pedometer Also Helps Those Who Work Out

If you regularly work out but are not seeing the outcomes you want, a pedometer can help. The pedometer will remind you that you need to be more active throughout the day. And the more you move, the higher amount of calories you will burn.

Step by Step Plan on Using the Pedometer

Objective: increase the number of steps you normally take by 7500 – the average increase that most people achieved.

Walk Your Way To Weight Loss

Step 1: Determine how much activity you are presently getting. In order to do that, place the pedometer on your waist for at least three days – from the time you wake up and get out of bed until the time you go to sleep at night. Do what you usually do. If you don't normally take a walk at lunch, don't start now. Measure at least one weekend day, since the levels of your activity vary from weekdays.

Step 2: Compute your baseline by getting the average of your step counts for 3 days.

Step 3: Print the chart and mark the range that includes your baseline number.

Step 4: Determine your goal by adding 7500 steps to your baseline.

Step 5: Check your chart and look for the number closest to your goal.

Step 6: Analyze the data you have collected. These include your initial goal, the steps you need to take to achieve this goal, and how long it will take. If you need more time, take it.

Step 7: After achieving your initial goal, continue with your activity to achieve your ultimate goal.

Step 8: Maintain your ultimate goal for eight weeks. If you are no longer getting the results from this activity level, you can increase your daily steps. If you don't have enough time for more walking, concentrate on increasing your intensity instead by including more hills or going faster.

Additional Facts about Pedometer

A person only needs 10,000 steps to successfully lose weight. It might seem impossible to achieve it, but actually it will take you only one and a half hours of brisk walking to complete 10,000 steps. This is not hard at all, right? Also, walking outdoors benefits your health in several ways: it provides a fresh air intake, refreshes your skin, puts you in a better mood and tones your muscles.

Since walking is not as intensive as cycling or jogging, you need to walk longer in order to burn the same amount of calories that you would if you perform intensive training. 30 minutes of walking normally take around 4,000 steps. You can burn about two hundred calories. If you want to lose some pounds, you need to walk intensively. By doing this, your heart beat rate will remain at the level which benefits fat burning. If you cannot do the 1 ½ hours of walking per day, divide the time in half – for instance walk to and from your work.

Chapter 10 – Walking to Lose Weight Success Stories

Here are some success stories that might get you motivated and start with your own walking program.

Less Effort, Better Results

Annette Burke a 39 year old executive assistant who believes that even with less effort you can get better results.

Results:

- Increased activity by 9950 steps each day
- Lose weight – 5 pounds
- Cholesterol level lowered by 24 points
- Reduce one mile walk time by more than three minutes

She has been biking and spinning on and off for four years. She was surprised when the results that she wanted for many years can be achieved only by walking. According to her, it was very easy, all she needs to do in the morning is to slip the pedometer and walk.

Tips that helped her succeed:

- Parking her car farther away to her destination.
- Taking the longest route to other offices
- Instead of using the elevator, use the stairs

- Carrying out regular "step checks" helped her to focus on her target, so there is no need for her to cope up with the steps she need after work.

Getting the Results After 3 Weeks

Diane was surprised at how many steps she could do without engaging into any structured exercise.

Results:

- Increased activity by 6051 steps each day
- Lose 4 pounds
- Lose four inches off hips, thighs and waist
- Cut one mile walk time by more than five minutes

Tips that helped Diane Succeed:

- Taking notes of her activity. Record some creative ways on how to acquire more steps. Keeping a record of all her accomplishments motivated her to continue.
- Making use of her extra time by taking a walk rather than sitting while waiting for her next activity.
- Making new opportunities. When stopping to get gas, instead of waiting she would walked home while her husband drove the car.
- Socializing on the move. Instead of sitting and eating, she now prefers to walk and talk with her friends.
- Making it fun. To complete her final step count, Diane would dance to the music on the radio or TV.

After 3 weeks she received her major bonus. Started to feel

more tone and she loves the comments she hears from others. According to some of her friends, she was looking slimmer. She is now adopting other healthful habits, like drinking more water rather than diet cola to keep her hydrated.

Having a Hard Time Focusing on Steps

Rod Yerk a 50 year old maintenance supervisor achieved the weight that he wants within 3 weeks. A few days after engaging into walking pedometer program to lose weight, he's enthusiasm was challenged by an overwhelming job activities, making it hard for him to focus on steps during the day. So he finds ways on how he can complete the number of steps needed outside of work.

Results:

- Increased activity by 5405 steps everyday
- Lose 9 pounds
- Lost 4 ¼ inches off hips, thighs and waist
- Reduced total cholesterol by 17 points
- Reduced LDL cholesterol by 16 points

Tips that helped Rod achieved his goal

- Taking his pet dog for more frequent walks.
- Doing household chores more often.

After 3 weeks, Rod lost three pounds and increase stamina. He also cut down on his meal portions. After the pretest evaluation, Rod was only able to walk ¾ of a mile, but after eight weeks, he walked a full mile easily.

Breaking and Making New Habits

Brenda Miller is a 47 Manufacturing Coordinator

With the help of the pedometer, counting steps became part of her everyday routine and her past sedentary habits started to improve.

Results:

- Increased activity by 7888 steps each day
- Lose 12 pounds
- Lost five inches off hips, thighs and waist
- Reduced cholesterol by 72 points

Tips that helped Brenda achieved her goal

- While waiting for her flight at the airport, she walks around rather than sitting.
- During long drives, she makes frequent stops and walk for 15 minutes.
- Common errands at home have helped her to make more steps. If she doesn't have anything heavy to carry, she would walk to the drugstore, supermarket and video store.
- She encouraged her son or husband to join her on walks. It is the best way to connect with your family and divert your attention from passive activities like watching TV.

She started noticing the change in the first week. According to her, she feels better about herself, knowing that she is doing something to lose weight and improver her energy level. Six months later, she is still using her pedometer to maintain her weight and energy level.

A Little Help From Linda's Friends

Linda Frey is a 43 year old customer service specialist and she wants to lose some weight through walking.

Results:

- Increased activity by 5496 steps everyday
- Lose 7 pounds
- Lost 4 ¼ inches off thighs, hips and waist
- Lowered cholesterol by 32 points

After realizing that her office job only afforded her 3500 steps the maximum during office hours, Linda had to find ways to reach her daily goal of 10,000 steps.

Tips that helped her reached her goal

Walking rather than driving to her destinations was a good start.

To add more steps, she started her own walking club. Everyday, she would request someone to walk with her. The support and eagerness of her close friends were the best motivators.

Linda not just loses weight, but she also had more energy

and can climb stairs with our puffing and huffing. And by staying away off the couch, she noticed that she can keep off the weight while still eating the same amount of food.

Chapter 11 – Walking Workout Plans and How it Works

You might not know it but the secret to finally lose those unwanted fats is by simple workout known as walking. Walking burns around 4 calories in a minute, and according to science they add up to lose weight and keep it off. As compared to couch sitters, walkers have less overall flab and also have less bellies. According to Whitney M. Cole, a professional trainer in Los Angeles who heads a powerful-walk exercises in the Hollywood Hills, walkers also can melt more calories at the same time can firm more muscle fibers. To achieve the steps that you require to lose weight, burn fat and stay fit, here are some walking programs that can help you. You can mix and match these programs to achieve the 150 minute a week target that will help keep you in shape.

15 – Minute Lunchtime Quickie

Walking is considered as the best way to ward off job blob. One reason is that through walking you can burn 50 extra calories a day, the equivalent of a steady 15-minute stroll. This can help you determine if you lose weight or not. As compared to rigorous workout, power walking won't provide you the post-exercise munchies, this is according to the study done from the Loughborough University in the UK.

Look for a place to order your lunch that is about 8 minute walk. Call in your order and inform them that you will pick up your order. Do this everyday to accumulate 45 minutes to an hour of exercise without even exerting effort. If you want a butt-firming boost, squeeze your glutes while walking.

Walk Your Way To Weight Loss

40- Minute De-Stressing Stroll

The best way to combat brain drain is just put one foot in front of the other. Even a 10-minute jaunt removes anxiety and improves mood. To prevent your mind from racing, repeat on your own, "one-two" as your feet land. To recharge, walk to the beat of the music.

30 – Minute Burner and Butt Firmer

In order to lose fat, there is no need for you to go up the hills or hit the gas. Exaggerating your stride length strengthen your butt and quads to work harder. Alternate 1 minute of moderate walking and 1-minute of exaggerated lunges or strides to increase your sizzle.

Suggested Activities for 30 minutes

0 minutes – 4 minutes	to warm up walk at a moderate speed.
4 minutes – 9 minutes	Power surge for 1 minute, take exaggerated strides that are 6 to 12 inches longer than standard. Keep a tall posture, look straight ahead. Alternate with 1-minute recovery walks carried out at a moderate speed.
9 minutes – 13 minutes	Power surge for 1 minute with walking thrusts. Lunge forward with your right leg, bend both knees ninety degrees, then slightly rise as you carry your left

Walk Your Way To Weight Loss

	leg forward into a lunge. Keep low to fry your thighs. Alternate with 1-minute moderate speed recovery walks.
13 minutes – 17 minutes	Switch between 1 minute of exaggerated strides and 1 minute at a moderate speed.
17 minutes – 21 minutes	Alternate between 1 minute of walking thrusts and 1 minute at a moderate speed.
21 minutes – 30 minutes	Repeat 13 minutes – 21 minutes activities. Cool down.

20 to 40 Minute Fat Burner

To increase the calories that you can burn, replace 5-minute chunks of your
normal loop with these slow walk to run intervals. Within 20 minutes you will burn 147 calories rather than 70 calories.

0 minute – 5 minutes	Walk at a moderate speed to warm up.
5 minutes – 10 minutes	Repeat the following cycle 5 times: For 20 seconds walk briskly. Jog for 20 secs. Sprint for 20 secs.
10 minutes – 12 minutes	Walk fast.
12 minutes – 17 minutes	Continue with your walk-jog-sprint routine

Walk Your Way To Weight Loss

17 minutes – 20 minutes   Walk fast.

Repeat this routine if you have more time for a 40-minute exercise.

45 Minute Treadmill Trimmer

If you are worrying about the traffic, darkness or weather, treadmill is the best
excuse. As you increase your speed, you become fit which is also a good
motivator. Lee Scott an expert in walking workout also suggests starters to use
the treadmill to lose more than 150 calories within half an hour. Start with a
comfortable speed. As you go along increase the speed at 0.6 mph. For each
succeeding phase, increase your speed intervals by 0.2 mph. The amount of
calories you burn will depend on your weight, workout duration and walking –
speed.

Reverse Your Fat-Burning Switch

You could lose weight this month by adding high-intensity walks to your daily routine. You will get rid more fats during and after your cardiovascular workouts. And there are choices to fit everyone's needs – a ten minute routine during busy days and an indoor option during rainy days. For optimum results, do at least twenty minutes of high-intensity walking (any combination of the workouts on this part or any of the stair or hill routines in the following parts – the longer walks will slim you down quicker) on three nonconsecutive days a week. Do moderate-intensity activity on alternate days, for about thirty minutes every session.

Drop-It-Fast Sprint

You can go farther if you walk faster and the more weight you will lose. Here is a fun walking plan that gets rid of 175 calories. The workout will start with a warm up routine. When done with the warm up for five minutes, walk for ten minutes at a fast pace. Take note of how far you went. Then walk briskly back to the office, gradually slowing your speed to cool down as you get near to where you start. Every time you do this routine, aim to walk faster and go farther than where you start.

Megacalorie Burner

This type of walking workout is perfect for the weekend for 60 plus minutes. This can crank up your post-exercise calorie burn almost fivefold, as compared to a 30 minute walk. It only means you can burn around 350 calories during your walk. This can likewise get you in shape to achieve a bigger objective, like half marathon or a multi day fund raising walk. It is also a social way to lose weight. Plan your routine so you meet up with friends, and walk together. This will keep you from getting bored.

Belly-Busting Walk

You can do this walking working out for ten plus minutes. This high-intensity workout such as this one can lose 5 times more belly fat than moderate-intensity routine. To achieve your goal on shaping your abs, apply these tips while walking:

Concentrate on drawing your abs in toward your spine. Maintain the tightening throughout your walk, but don't hold your breath.

Walk like your legs extend up above your navel. As one leg swings back and forward, the hip should follow. Your lower torso to spin is This slight hip twist can cause your lower torso to spin, this will help produce additional ab muscles to tighten your midsection quicker.

Super Fat Blast

This is a ten minute walking workout. Build up the momentum with digestion-roaring bursts of high-impact tasks. You will burn around 70% more calories than if you walked at a steady speed.

Rev Energy and Brighten Your Mood

Each time you need a quick pick-me up, try one of these sequences. A stroll for 10-minute can recharge your energy instantly by boosting circulation. Go for 30 minutes and you could get a 85% energy boost, this is according to research. And to really energize your brain and body, try these stimulating walks that will get your senses and mind working. The good feeling may actually last for 12 hours. It does not matter whether you want to lose weight, burn fat or get fit, these workouts can really help.

Happiness Walk

Rev up your mind and body with a simple walk that includes these stress-busting methods. The longer you walk, the more benefits you can get.

Step 1
Concentrate on your feet. Your feet should feel the ground as each foot rolls from heel to toe. Try to be conscious of your steps for two to three minutes.

Step 2
Then divert your attention to breathing. To stand upright lift your torso and increase lung space. As you inhale, think as if you are drawing in renewed energy. Exhale pain and tiredness. Allow fresh life flow into your cells and lungs.

Step 3
Talk to yourself mentally. Imagining fresh air in, bad air out as you breathe can help you keep focused.

Brainpower Booster

You can do this walking workout 20 minutes or below. Changing the direction you walk – backward, sideways or forward – keeps your mind awake, increase the amount of calorie you can burn, and activates some most of the time seldom used muscles, like your inner and outer thighs. This workout is best done on a school track usually around ¼ mile.

The Routine:

Lap 1
Begin at the start of the curved part of the track. To warm up for a full lap, walk as you normally would do.

Lap 2
Turn sideways so to have your right foot in front. Shuffle or sidestep around the curved part of the track. Walk backward on the straight path. Sidestep through the next curve with left foot in front. Walk forward on the straight path.

Lap 3
Do the lap 2 again, walking sideways, backward, sideways, and forward.

Lap 4
Walk forward, slow down to cool down. If you use a ¼ mile track, this is a 1-mile walk. To extend this, you can do more laps or work up to doing half or even full laps of each sort of walking.

Find a Place with Lots of Trees

This is a 5-minute walking workout. To boost your energy and improve your mood gets a dose of nature for five minutes. If you work out in a natural environment and go longer (a stroll during lunch break in a park or an all-day hike in the hills), you can improve your attention and memory 20% more than you can by strolling in an urban environment. It's because there are less distractions and it is more relaxing.

Firm Your Thighs, Butt, And Arms

By including some toning techniques or exercises in your routine, you can transform walks into total body workouts and shape your butt and legs even faster. Focus on every part of your body area 2 or 3 times a week. For instance, do the sculpt all over workout one or two times a week, and do an upper and lower body routine on alternate days. Don't use the same muscle groups on back-to-back days. To speed up firming, carry out walking routines from other areas on in-between days to burn fat and display your sexy muscles.

Double-Duty Toner

Use a pair of walking poles. Study shows they can boost the burning of calories by up to 48% and get your core and arms involved for firming the entire body. The poles likewise lessen the effect on your joints.

Treadmill Booty Blast

This is a 25 minute walking workout. Work out your glutes, by doing treadmill routine. You can also do one or two five minute hill climbs for a shorter session.

Arm Shaper

This is a 20 minute walking workout. Get an exercise band and do the arms exercise while you walk to firm your upper body. Start with four minutes of easy walking. Then increase your speed to a moderate intensity, and perform the first exercise for 25 reps. When you are done, drape the resistance band around your neck and increase your speed to a brisk pace, as if you are in a hurry, for two minutes. Do the 25 rep toning / two min. brisk-walking breaks until you have completed all the workouts. Cool down with four minutes of casual walking. You can do the moves a little bit difficult by putting your hands closer to each other so you need less band, or simpler by separating hands for more relaxed.

Butt Firmer

This is a 16 minute walking workout. Walking uphill produces 25% more muscle fibers for quicker firming as compared to strolling on flat terrain. For better result, look for a hill that takes two to two and half minutes to climb and do this workout. Warm up at a slow pace for five to ten minutes. Then walk up and down the hill, followed by two minutes of brisk walking on a level surface. Repeat this workout depending on your desired length. Finish with five minutes of casual walking to settle down.

Sculpt All Over

This is a 25 to 40 minute walking workout. During this workout, you will spread strength moves as you walk, for heart plus toning. Using the lottery approach workout, write at least 9 no-equipment strength workout on pieces of paper. Exercises vary to hit all important muscle groups, like walking lunges, tricep dips, power jumps, planks and bench push-ups. Place them in a jar and pick three out before a walk. Warm up at a simple pace for three to five minutes, then walk briskly for five to ten minutes. Stop and perform one of the strength moves for ten reps. Repeat the brisk walking, followed by the next strength move. Do this again to complete the final move. Cool down for five minutes at an easy pace.

Indoor Leg Toner

This walking workout will only take 5 minutes. You can perform this quick workout anywhere where there are stairs to increase the amount of calories burned. Walk up and down one flight normally. Then, slowly walk up sideways, crossing your bottom foot over the top. Keep your head up. Walk down normally. Do this routine again, facing the other direction. Step up on the first stair, then down, beginning with the right foot (right up, left up, right down, left down) ten times. Do this again, starting with the left foot. Climb stairs two steps at a time, come down fast using each step. Run up, walk down normally. Repeat the last two routine 4 times. At bottom, position right foot on the first or second step, bend knees, and lower into a lunge. Keep right knee over your ankle as you do so. Push off with right foot to start again. Do this again using left leg. Alternate legs for twenty lunges all in all.

Chapter 12 - Additional Facts About Walking

The Logic Behind Arm Swing While Walking

Swinging of arms while walking is a natural motion. Each arm swings with the motion of the opposing leg. The angular momentum of the body is reduced as the arm swing in an opposing directing with respect to the lower limb, balancing the rotational movement produced during walking. Even though the pendulum like movement of arms is not important for walking, recent studies showed that the arm swing improves the energy efficiency and stability in human locomotion. Those positive impacts of arm swing have been used in sports, particularly in sprinting and racewalking.

Kinematics

The studies on the importance of arm swing include analysis of bipedal walking models and treadmill experiments on human. In bipedal walking, the leg swing produces an angular momentum that is balanced by the ground reaction moments on the stable foot. Swinging arms produce an angular momentum in the opposing direction of lower limb rotation, decreasing the total angular momentum of the body. The lower angular momentum of the body results in a decrease in the ground reaction moment on the stable foot. Frequency or amplitude of arm movements is identified by the gait, which means that the swing motion is adaptive to distresses and changing conditions. As the walking pace increases, the amplitude of the arm swing likewise increases. The frequency of the movement of the arm changes with the speed as well. Studies showed that at speed 0.8 m/s or lower, the frequency ratio between the leg and arm movements is 2:1 while speeding higher than this the ratio becomes 1:1.

Theories About Walking

Stability

Both experiments on force plate and simulations of skeletal models correspond to that since the overall angular momentum is reduced with the counterbalancing swing of arms with respect to the lower-limb the free arm swing restricts the ground reaction moments effective on the stable foot during walking. In short, a subject requires less reaction moment applied by the ground surface when walking includes arm swing. Having a less need for a reaction moment means that the friction force between the ground surface and the stable foot does not have to be as high as it would when there is no arm swing involved. Less need for the friction force, is the possible result of the arm swing.

Saves Energy

Whether arm swing is the result of the rotation of torso or an active movement that needs energetic muscle work has been an important topic on arm swing that might clarify its function and benefit. The present study focused on the energy used during walking showed that low pace arm swing is an inactive movement controlled by the kinematics of the torso, the movement is the same with the pendula suspended from the shoulders. The upper extremity of the muscle works controlled by the brain, only takes place when there is distress and restores that natural movement. But, at a faster pace, the passive movement is not enough to explain the amount of the swing noticed in the experiments. The work of the active muscle increases together with the walking speed. In spite the fact that a certain amount of energy is used for the arm movement, the overall energy consumption drops, which means that the arm swing still decreases the cost of walking. That decreased in the energy is up to 12% at particular walking speeds, a great saving.

Evolution

Another major topic of interest when it comes to walking is the inter-limb coordination, questioning whether the gait of a person is based on quadruped locomotion. A recent study shows that inter-limb coordination while walking is organized in the same way to that in the cat, pointing out the view that arm swing could be the remaining function from quadruped gait. The former studies, was corroborated with another work on the arm movements control mechanisms during walking, showing that CPG or central pattern generator could be involved in the cyclic arm swing. But, these observations do not mean vestigiality of arm swing, which was debated in 2003 after the evidences on the function of arm swing in bipedal locomotion was released.

The Importance of Arm Swing in Athlete's Performance

Energy efficiency of arm swing and its ability in controlling the momentum of the body have been used in sports. Runners make use of the contribution of arm swing on the linear momentum to get a higher forward acceleration. The race walkers are likewise using the arm swing for its energy efficiency. Instead of the rhythmic motions while walking, swinging the arms appropriately helps athlete performs in various disciplines. Swinging the arm forward can improve the performance of the athlete in standing long jump during the onset of the jump. During landing the back and forth swinging of the arms is needed since it can control the linear momentum of the body. Use of arms in adjusting the linear and rotational momentum is also a common practice in gymnastics and somersaulting.

Walking in Robotics

The robotics researchers partly created the literature on the arm swing as the stability in locomotion is an important challenge particularly in humanoid robots. Although lots of humanoid robots maintained fixed equilibrium while walking which does not need arm swing, arm movements have been included in the present humanoid robot walking in great equilibrium. The motion of the arms just like the pendulum is likewise used in passive dynamic walkers, an instrument that can walk on its own.

Neuromechanical Considerations

Knowing the underlying neural mechanisms on the organization of rhythmic arm movement and its coordination with the lower limb will allow the development of effective strategies for spinal cord injury rehabilitation and stroke patients. The rhythmic arm movements for various tasks – arm swing while walking, arm swing while standing, and cycling arms while standing – were analyzed in this perspective and the results aimed at the common central control mechanism.

Walking Speed

The speed in walking will depend on the person's preference. Normally, a person walks at about 1.4m/s. But there are some who are capable of walking at speeds from 0 to up to 2.5m/s. The majority of us preferred to walk only a small range within these speeds. People find exceptionally slow or fast speeds uncomfortable, not unless needed such as when working out to burn fats. Horses have likewise showed normal, narrow distribution of walking speed within a given gait, which means that the process of choosing the speed may follow the same patterns across species. The preferred walking speed has significant clinical applications as a sign of mobility and independence. For instance, elderly or those who are suffering from osteoarthritis prefer to walk more slowly. Increasing the preferred walking speed has therefore been an important clinical goal in these populations.

Some factors that can contribute to the speed selection are as follows psychological, mechanical, physiological and energetic. Also, people face a tradeoff between several costs-related with various walking speeds and choose a speed with less costs. For instance, people may need to reach their destination fast, so they choose to walk fast, and metabolic rate, joint stress or muscle force, which are minimized at slow walking speeds. Generally increasing motivation, metabolic efficiency or value of time may result to people walking at fast speed. On the other hand, joint pain, metabolic rate, aging, incline, visual gain and instability cause people to walk more slowly.

Chapter 13 - Joining a Walking Club

Starting a walking club requires some effort and provides great rewards. It is one way of removing boredom while walking and boost motivation. Before you know it you are walking toward better health.

Since walking does not require special skills or tools, it has become the most preferred form of physical activity in the United States. If you enjoy walking, why not invite others to walk along with you. Getting support from others by walking together can help you adhere to your health and fitness goals. Creating a walking group is not that hard, and the results are worth it.

Benefits of Joining a Walking Club

You are aware of the benefits of walking. Here are some of the benefits if you join a walking club.

- Socialization
- Accountability
- Safety
- Motivation

A walking club will consist of walkers of all ages and social backgrounds. One of the benefits of joining the club is that you can meet different kinds of people, many of them you might not have come across in your everyday life so the social aspect of being a member of the club can widen your scopes. Also, if you are a starter, you will not feel the odd one since there are other beginners walking with you, thus creates a bond that might result in new friendships. Also, there will be experienced walkers who can give advice and some helpful walking tips. They will likewise be able to inform you the best stores to purchase your gear and other clubs usually have some sort of connection with certain youth hostels etc. and outdoor stores where you will benefit from discounted prices and rates.

A walking club will likewise provide you the opportunity to venture out to different walking areas and to check out places you may not otherwise have visited. One of the best attractions about walking is that you will experience something different and new every time you head out for a walk and also when you are walking along different trails in other places of the country or even further. And as compared to non-organized groups which can cause problems if there are walkers of different levels of expertise and fitness, most of the walking clubs have separate walks to suit the different levels of ability. For instance, group a may include the most experienced walkers and they may end up going for a 20 mile walk, on hilly terrain while group d may include the beginners with an 8 mile walk on flat grounds.

Encourage Others to Join the Club

Spreading the word about the club is a good start in building a walking group. You can discuss the ideas and goals of the club with your friends and family members and neighbors. You can use social media sites like Twitter or Facebook to reach out those who are interested in joining your club.

Maybe you choose to recruit your colleagues. If this is the case, you can discuss with your employer the idea of having a friendly workplace competition. There are lots of big companies that challenge their employee to a pedometer contest. The group that gets the most steps takes home the prize or a recognition from the company. Or, keep track of the time the group consumes on certain activity and see which group comes out on the top each week.

Get Organized

As soon as you have gathered members for your walking club, hold a kick off meeting. Ask for their email address, phone numbers and other contact information, so you can stay in touch about events and keep each other motivated. You can also build your group website, so it is much easier for you to contact others.

Things you can discuss with your walking group:
- Your walking schedule
- The route to take
- The distance to cover
- What to do in case of bad weather
- When and where to meet
- The speed to walk
- Whether to walk indoors or outdoors

Your walking club should be flexible to accommodate weather, illness, work schedules or other factors that may occur. If you have recruited lots of people, consider dividing them according to their walking experience and level, availability, fitness goals or other factors.

On the other hand, if the members of your walking club are at various fitness levels, you may motivate and encourage each other by working out together. Staying motivated is one of the important factors in achieving your goals and keeps you fit for the long period of time. So depend on your walking partners for support, particularly on those days when you feel like skipping your walking exercises.

Keep the Momentum High

Once you have established your walking routine, find ways to maintain and boost motivation. You can choose a name for your walking club, set group goals and enter charity walking events to increase walking intensity or time. The camaraderie you get in a walking club and the shared fitness success can help you achieve your desired weight and stay fit. Reasons in Joining a Walking Club

If you are searching for ways to get fit, lose weight, burn fat, boost your energy and have fun, joining a walking group could be the best way to make your wellness objectives into reality. The walking groups or clubs are becoming popular and are increasing in number. Here are some reasons why you should join the walking club and the things it can do for you.

1. Walking is very beneficial for your body. Let's begin with the basics. Regular walking has a positive effect on your heart health by decreasing your cholesterol and lowering your blood pressure, reducing your risk of having heart attacks and strokes. Walking can likewise boost your bone density and it improves the overall quality of life.
2. You will adhere with it. The club will help you stick with your plan. If you intend to lose weight, the club

will help you achieve your goal. Statistics show that around 70% of people who start an exercise plan quit within the first 6 months. The reason for this is that they are not motivated.

The walking club can help that little bit of positive peer pressure that will help you stand up, go out and on your feet. People are more encouraged and likely to show up and join if they are part of a group activity.

3. Lose weight. Walking for 30 minutes eliminate around 125 calories. If this is not enough, just imagine if you walk five days a week for the entire year, you will lose around 32,500 calories and that is more than 5 kg of fat. The best fat burning effects of walking starts at about 30 to 40 minutes after the start of the walk, thus if you walk for more than thirty minutes at a stretch, you will lose more weight.

4. Clubs are fun. Most of the walking clubs have social atmosphere. It feels like a special time or free time to spend it with people that you enjoy as compared to exercising.

Your friends and neighbors can join the club, or you can sign up on your own and meet new friends that have the same interests like yours. If you are in a club, you can have a good chat while you are walking.

5. It will boost your mood. A study shows that group exercise releases endorphins also referred to as the happy hormones. These hormones scan help you transform something that seems to be a boring activity into a real pleasure. Also, some experts say that walking in a good company and in pleasant

environment helps you sleep well and reduce the risk of having anxiety and depression.

6. Clubs are safe. If you walk along with your group mates you can feel safe walking in new areas of your community and at night without worrying about your safety.

Discover new areas of your hood. Most of the walking clubs explore various routes and terrains, so while you are getting fit, you are likewise getting more familiar with the locations in your own community.

Stay Motivated

There are lots of people who make elaborate plans to lose weight. One of the biggest hurdles for a person to lose weight is how to stay motivated to achieve your goals. As discussed in the previous chapters, having a regular walking routine can help you a lot in losing weight. If your goals are not realistic, you will fail.

You should set your daily routine. You should set your target of losing 50 lbs in eight weeks. If you think this is possible then stick to your plan of achieving it. You can also ask the help of your friend who is also trying to lose weight and is engaged in walking workout. This will make things easier for you to complete the routine every day. There is no need for you to make big changes to your everyday routine.

Diet and Exercise

Although walking is very effective in losing weight , but diet and exercise can also make things easier to lose weight. Your body requires time to recover between workouts, taking the right food is very important. Pushing yourself too hard will only hurt you.

Avoiding doing the same thing every day can help you stay motivated. Keep everything you do fresh by not always walking on the same location. Look for another location where you can do your walking workout. This will help you complete your routine without feeling bored and tired.

When it comes to food make sure that you eat healthy food. There is no need to stay away from foods that you love to eat. Keeping everything in moderation is important. You can eat pizza but make sure that you take the right amount.

Summary of Facts and Benefits

On average, a minute of walking can actually extend your life by 1.5 to 2 minutes.

Walking an additional 20 minutes every day will burn around 7 lbs of body fat each year.

To get rid of 1 plain M & M candy, you should walk the full length of the football field. Before eating M&M, think about that and decide if you really want to dip your hand into a bowl of M&M or not.

Make sure that you walk longer at a moderate pace every

Walk Your Way To Weight Loss

day, it is about 40 minutes of walking at 60 to 65% maximum heart rate. This is perfect for losing weight.

Shorter walk at fast pace for 20-25 minutes are perfect for your lungs and heart healthy.

Walking everyday provides the following health benefits:

- Burns body fat
- Elevates mood
- Helps control addictions to nicotine, alcohol, caffeine, and other drugs
- Helps control and prevent diabetes
- Helps control your appetite
- Helps prevent and/or reduce depression
- Helps promote restful sleep
- Helps relieve stress
- Improves efficiency of your heart and lungs
- Improves flexibility
- Improves mental alertness and memory
- Improves posture
- Improves your self-esteem
- Increases your energy
- Lowers high blood pressure
- Promotes healthier skin due to increased circulation
- Promotes intestinal regularity
- Improves your metabolism so you are burning calories quicker, even while you rest
- Reduces risk of some forms of cancer including colorectal, prostrate, and breast
- Reduces stiffness in your joints due to inactivity or arthritis

- Relieves most cases of chronic backache
- Slows aging
- Spurs intellectual creativity and problem solving
- Keep your bones strong and reduces bone density loss in older women

Lots of people preferred walking instead of jogging or running because it produces less on the joints, knees, ankles and hips. Don't forget to warm up properly before and cool down after every walking workout.

Conclusion

Thank you again for purchasing this book!

I hope this book was able to help you to realize how easy it is to lose weight effectively by walking.

The next step is to try incorporating walking to your routine as soon as you can.

Finally, if you enjoyed this book, please take the time to share your thoughts and post a review on Amazon. We do our best to reach out to readers and provide the best value we can. Your positive review will help us achieve that. It'd be greatly appreciated!

Thank you and good luck!

Check Out My Other Books

Below you'll find some of my other popular books that are popular on Amazon and Kindle as well. Simply click on the links below to check them out. Alternatively, you can visit my author page on Amazon to see other work done by me.

Coconut Oil for Skin Care & Hair Loss: A Step by Step Guide for Using Virgin Coconut Oil for Youthful Skin and Healthy Hair

http://amzn.to/1p0GwGC

COCONUT OIL & WEIGHT LOSS FOR BEGINNERS: Proven Secrets of Virgin Coconut Oil & Quick Weight Loss

Or go to http://amzn.to/1jqdy3R

Walk Your Way To Weight Loss 2nd edition: The Ultimate Guide On How To Lose Weight, Burn Fat & Stay Thin With Walking

http://amzn.to/1jOHpgy

Quick, Easy, Healthy Snack Ideas for Kids: Low cost, Friendly, Quick, & Delicious Everyday Snacks for Kids

http://amzn.to/1grvURn

Oil Pulling Therapy For Beginners: Detoxify & Heal Your Mouth, Teeth, Gums & Body With Coconut Oil Through Natural Oil Pulling

http://amzn.to/SBD0Xb

Healing Babies and Children with Aromatherapy for Beginners: Proven Steps on How to Use Essential Oils and Aromatherapy to Care for Babies and Children

http://amzn.to/TOHJHs

Carb Cycling for Fast Easy Weight Loss: Proven Steps on How to Lose Stubborn Belly Fat, Live Healthy & Build Muscle for Life!

http://amzn.to/THn8Vl

BEAUTY PRODUCTS FOR BEGINNERS: The Secret Homemade Recipe Guide Using Essential Oils for Natural Skin Care, Hair Care and Body Care

http://amzn.to/1nVvwNw

Body Lotions For Beginners: The Ultimate Guide to Making All Natural Body Lotions for Glowing, Youthful, Vibrant Skin

http://amzn.to/S3XlWh

Container Gardening For Beginners: The Essential Basics Of Container Gardening To Growing Fruits, Vegetables & Herbs In The Smallest Spaces!

http://amzn.to/1oLb2po

The Ultimate Guide to Companion Gardening for Beginners: How to Use Companion Plants for a Successful Flower or Vegetable Garden

http://amzn.to/1hYzeEl

The Ultimate Guide to Vegetable Gardening for Beginners: How to Grow Your Own Healthy Organic Vegetables All Year Round!

http://amzn.to/1lqCCIK

The Ultimate Guide to Raised Bed Gardening for Beginners: How to Grow Flowers and Vegetables in Raised Beds for a Successful Garden

http://amzn.to/1nHY0ry

Greenhouse Gardening for Beginners: How to Grow Flowers and Vegetables Year-Round In Your Greenhouse

http://amzn.to/UEmOr2

Essential Oils Box Set #1: Healing Babies and Children with Aromatherapy for Beginners + Oil Pulling Therapy For Beginners

http://amzn.to/1yZoH0Q

Essential Box Set #2: Carb Cycling For Fast Easy Weight Loss + Walk Your Way to Weight Loss

http://amzn.to/Tu5xiL

Essential Box Set #3: Beauty Products For Beginners + Body Lotions For Beginners

http://amzn.to/1qnVLNQ

Essential Box Set #4: Coconut Oil & Weigh Loss for Beginners & Coconut Oil for Skin Care & Hair Loss

http://amzn.to/1iQQUlN

Essential Oils Box Set #5: Coconut Oil for Skin Care& Hair Loss+ Healing Babies and Children with Aromatherapy for Beginners + Beauty Products For + Body Lotions For Beginners+ Oil Pulling Therapy For Beginners

http://amzn.to/1qGPc6D

Essential Oils Box Set #6: Carb Cycling for Fast Easy Weight Loss+ Oil Pulling Therapy For Beginners + Walk Your Way To Weight Loss + Coconut Oil & Weight Loss For Beginners + Coconut Oil for Skin Care & Hair Loss

http://amzn.to/UXAAoz

Essential Box Set #7: Coconut Oil for Skin Care& Hair Loss + Oil Pulling Therapy For Beginners + Healing Babies and Children with Aromatherapy for Beginners

http://amzn.to/1nUdbg5

Garden Box Set #1: The Ultimate Guide to Raised Bed Gardening for Beginners + The Ultimate Guide to Vegetable Gardening for Beginners + The Ultimate Guide to Companion Gardening for Beginners + Greenhouse Gardening for Beginners + + Container Gardening For Beginners

http://amzn.to/1lZOssc

Gardening Box Set #2: Container Gardening For Beginners + Ultimate Guide to Companion Gardening for Beginners

http://amzn.to/1q4wma5

If the links do not work, for whatever reason, you can simply search for these titles on the Amazon website to find them.

Printed in Great Britain
by Amazon.co.uk, Ltd.,
Marston Gate.